# As

## Series "Fun Facts on Fruits and Vegetables"

## Written by Michelle Hawkins

# Asparagus

Series " Fun Facts on Vegetables"

By

Michelle Hawkins

Version 1.1 ~September 2020

Published by Michelle Hawkins at KDP

When Asparagus is planted, it takes three years to yields its 1ˢᵗ harvest.

Once harvested, Asparagus plants can produce for up to 15 years.

# Asparagus is part of the Lily family.

# It only has 20 calories per five spears of Asparagus.

# Once Asparagus is the size of a pencil, it can be harvested.

## China is the top producer of Asparagus in the world.

# Asparagus was first seen about 2,500 years ago in Greece.

# The word Asparagus means stalk or shoot.

# April is the most active month to harvest Asparagus.

## Other months to harvest Asparagus is from February to June.

**Asparagus is grown from a crown that you plant twelve inches deep in the ground.**

**You can harvest Asparagus for about six to seven weeks from the crown during spring and summer.**

# Asparagus is primarily grown in California, Michigan, and Washington state in the United States.

## Asparagus can be eaten raw or cooked.

# The hotter the temperature, the faster the Asparagus will be grown.

## As the temperature rises, you can go from every four to five days picking Asparagus to picking it daily.

# If storing Asparagus, cut off the ends and place upright in a jar with one inch of water.

## When storing, do not wash or soak the Asparagus.

## For best flavor, eat within two days.

# The world record was set in 2011 for eating 9 pounds and 52 ounces of Asparagus in ten minutes.

# Asparagus was introduced to the United States in the 17th century in New York by the Dutch.

**Asparagus is known to boost energy and help cleanse the urinary tract.**

**Asparagus is high in folate and Vitamin K, which helps blood to clot.**

**Asparagus have their own beetle called the Asparagus Beetle.**

**They will eat the foliage and bark on the Asparagus plant, making them undesirable.**

To harvest white Asparagus, you must take the dirt away of about nine inches and clip at the base.

Immediately after clipping, it is placed in a dark box to keep white.

Once white Asparagus is exposed to sunlight, it will turn pink.

# The best way to buy Asparagus is from your local farmer's market.

# Use it quickly after harvesting so that it doesn't lose its sweetness.

**The best Asparagus is tender, smooth, firm, straight, uniform in size with a tightly closed tip.**

**The worst Asparagus is thick stalks with a broad ridge, sunken or dull looking. This indicates an old Asparagus.**

# To cook, wash in cold water with brief cooking time.

# The best way to cook is to put stalks in boiling water and just to steam the tips.

# Asparagus originated in the Mediterranean.

# The 1st way that farmers used to combat weeds was with salt.

**Asparagus has no fat.**

**Asparagus has no cholesterol.**

**Asparagus is very low in sodium.**

# Asparagus contains the amino acid asparagine, which helps in brain development.

# This also helps you get rid of excess salt in your body.

Green Asparagus is what most
people buy and eat.

Purple Asparagus has high sugar
and low fiber content.

White Asparagus is the least
bitter.

# White Asparagus is made from a lack of sunlight.

**White Asparagus is the most labor-intensive. Asparagus must be cut as soon as it comes to the surface.**

# Greeks believed that Asparagus would heal toothaches and prevent bee stings.

# They described Asparagus as cleansing and healing.

# Asparagus can grow very quickly.

## If it has the 'perfect' environment, it has been know to grow six to ten inches in one day.

After harvest time, Asparagus plants become ferns with berries.

These ferns produce poisonous red berries.

By being a fern with berries, it makes the Asparagus have food and nutrition for the next year.

# Asparagus is high in anti-inflammatory nutrients.

# Also high in Vitamin C, beta-carotene, Vitamin E, Zine, manganese, and selenium

**Asparagus has high levels of antioxidants, which may help reduce heart disease.**

**The larger the Asparagus, the better the quality.**

# Asparagus plant roots can grow up to 78 inches under the ground.

# By giving the plant two years before harvesting, it becomes very beneficial to their lifetime.

A full-size Asparagus plant can grow up to five feet tall.

Asparagus is between seven to nine inches.

When harvesting Asparagus, cut or snap close to the ground, but not under the ground.

**China produces about seven million tons of Asparagus yearly.**

**Asparagus can be boiled, microwaved, cooked, fried, grilled, marinated, or pickled.**

# Other Books by Michelle Hawkins

**Series**

**Fun Facts on Birds for Kids.**

**Fun Fact on Fruits and Vegetables**

Made in United States
North Haven, CT
26 August 2022

23302606R00020